Our Wild Wetlands

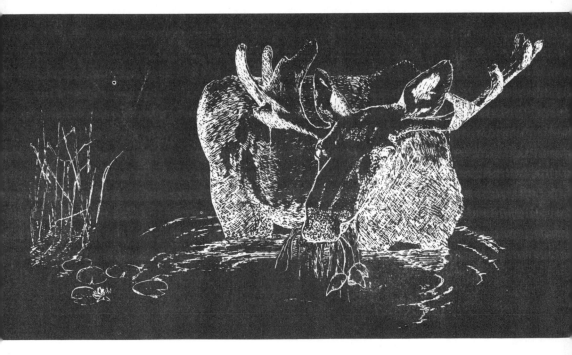

Our Wild Wetlands

by Sheila Cowing

Illustrated by Deborah Cowing

JULIAN MESSNER NEW YORK

Published by Julian Messner, a Simon & Schuster
Division of Gulf & Western Corporation, Simon &
Schuster Building, 1230 Avenue of the Americas,
New York, N.Y. 10020.

JULIAN MESSNER and colophon are trademarks of
Simon & Schuster, registered in the U.S. Patent
and Trademark Office.

Manufactured in the United States of America

Design by Alex D'Amato

Library of Congress Cataloging in Publication Data

Cowing, Sheila.
    Our wild wetlands.

    Includes index.
    SUMMARY: Discusses the value of wetlands, how they
were formed, the interdependence of plant and animal
life in bogs and marshes, and specific swamps in the
United States.
    1. Wetland ecology—Juvenile literature.
2. Wetlands—Juvenile literature. [1. Wetland
ecology.   2. Ecology]   I. Cowing, Deborah.
II. Title.
QH541.5.M3C68   574.5′26325′0973   80-17600
ISBN 0-671-33089-6

for Walt

ACKNOWLEDGMENT

The author wishes to express her appreciation to Walter A. Jones, Naturalist and Wetlands expert at the Environmental Education Center in Basking Ridge, N.J. for reading and checking the manuscript of this book.

Contents

1 What Good Are Wetlands?

For thousands of years people have wondered: What good are wetlands? Many were frightening places—hot, dark, smelly forests where solid ground wobbled underfoot and hidden creatures screamed and moaned. Some of the creatures were also terrifying, like the "devouring alligators" a traveler described in 1791. It was easy to get lost, since the way out was blocked by scummy pools or mazes of reed-lined channels. So people decided that wetlands were mosquito-infested wastelands—good for nothing. All over the world, millions of marshy acres were filled or drained for highways, farmland, used-car lots, factories or simply to make an area look neat.

However, in recent years, scientists have begun to look more carefully at wetlands. They have discovered that while wetlands are not tidy and clean, they are remarkably efficient. Working like sponges, they catch and hold water, checking floods, feeding streams in dry weather, and helping to maintain water levels in lakes and ponds. Inland, they are breeding grounds for fish and water birds. Along the coast, they are nurseries for many kinds of ocean fish. True, they are also nurseries for mosquitoes, but birds and fish will help control the insects if the wetland is healthy.

Wetlands are born when water is unable to drain off lowlands. They grow in every climate and every continent all over the world. They grow on flat or sunken places near the tops of mountains as well as in the bottoms of valleys.

People all over the world have many names for these soggy, wild places, but generally speaking, wetlands can be divided into three forms: bogs, marshes and swamps.

A bog was once a cold pond, perhaps dug by a glacier, that is slowly filling up with thick, spongy sphagnum moss. A true bog is fed only by the rain, and no streams flow in or out. Its water sits very still and changes very slowly. Very few animals and plants live in a bog.

Marshes, on the other hand, teem with life. Whether they spread along the edge of the sea or fill tiny hollows on the prairie late in spring, marshes look like seas of grass. Millions of water birds and animals live in the marsh grasses.

A swamp can support more life than any other wetland. Trees grow there as well as grasses and water plants, and the ground is strong enough for large land animals.

Different kinds of plants and animals live in each kind of wetland. But there are some places where all three forms blend, and plants and animals characteristic of one form may grow also in another.

A slow, natural process occurs in wetlands all over the earth. Many of them are dying lakes, and they are always changing. As soil is washed in by rain, a lake fills in from its shores and becomes a smaller pond. When washed-in soil builds up the pond bottom, grasses and reeds root, filling the shallows and attracting the fish, animals and birds that live in a marsh.

The grasses spread, and their roots grasp more and more mud until they have woven a thick mat. This soaks up so much of the marsh's water that water plants begin to die, and trees spring up at the edges of the marsh. The marsh is slowly becoming a swamp.

In the same way, the swamp will later become dry woods. The process of wetlands-becoming-dry lands takes hundreds, sometimes thousands of years, but it often follows this pattern: lake-pond-marsh-swamp-wet woods-woods.

Africa has more wetlands than any other continent.

In Asia, vast marshes and bogs stretch across Siberia, and wet salt flats blanket parts of India. Marshes formed in the delta where the Tigris and the Euphrates rivers empty into the Persian Gulf have been home to an unusual group of people for thousands of years.

Some Major Wetlands of the World

In northern Europe, the Pripet Marshes were the traditional border between Poland and the Soviet Union and have been crossed and re-crossed by soldiers throughout the long history of their battles with each other. Almost one-third of Finland is boggy.

In South America, huge swamps border the Amazon and the Orinoco rivers.

Far north, in northern Canada, Alaska and Siberia, where the sun shines all day and all night during the short, cool summers, the Arctic tundra thaws into a vast prairie marsh, spread with moss, lichens and tiny flowering plants.

Here, in the United States, we have more than 80 million acres of wetlands, some in every state. Some of these wetlands are tiny, just wet places alongside a highway with a few cattails and a redwinged blackbird. Others seem endless, like the dark, mysterious Okefenokee Swamp in Georgia and the great Bear River marshes north of Salt Lake City in Utah, where thousands of migrating water birds stop on their way and thousands more stay to nest.

Ecologists—the people who study a whole area to understand how plants and animals interact—believe we need our wetlands. If we destroy them, there will be fewer fish in the water and fewer birds in the air. We may even be foreshadowing the end of life, because our wetlands help regulate our freshwater supply.

What good are wetlands? They are good for life.

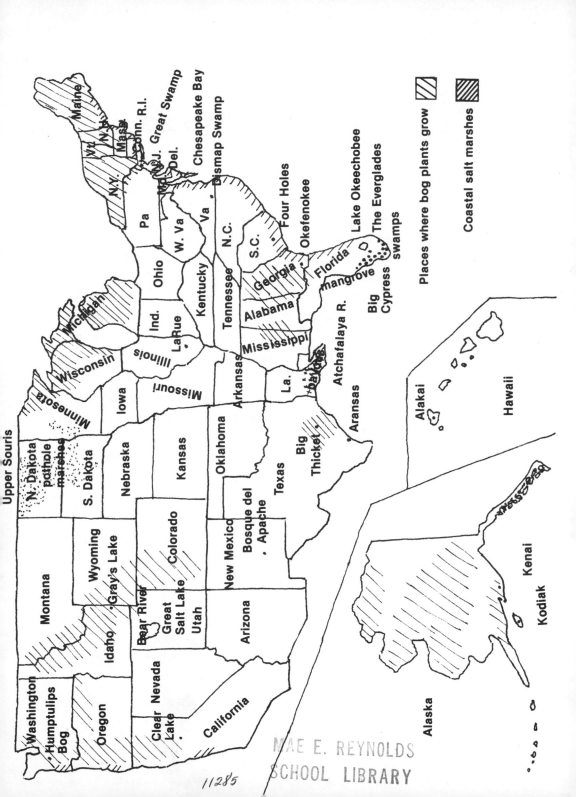

Places where bog plants grow

Coastal salt marshes

Upper Souris

Maine
Vt.
N.H.
Mass.
Conn. R.I.
N.J. Great Swamp
N.Y.
Del.
Md.
Chesapeake Bay
Pa
Dismap Swamp
W. Va
Va.
Ohio
Kentucky
N.C.
Four Holes
Ind.
Tennessee
S.C.
Okefenokee
LaRue
Lake Okeechobee
Michigan
Georgia
Florida
The Everglades
Illinois
Alabama
mangrove
Big Cypress swamps
Wisconsin
Mississippi
Atchafalaya R.
Minnesota
Iowa
Missouri
Arkansas
La.
bayous
Aransas
N. Dakota pothole marshes
Nebraska
Kansas
Oklahoma
Big Thicket
Alakai
Hawaii
S. Dakota
Wyoming
Colorado
New Mexico
Texas
Bosque del Apache
Gray's Lake
Montana
Bear River
Great Salt Lake
Utah
Arizona
Kenai
Kodiak
Idaho
Clear Lake
Nevada
California
Alaska
Washington
Humptulips Bog
Oregon

MAE E. REYNOLDS
SCHOOL LIBRARY

11285

2 Long Before People

Long before any people lived on earth, wetlands were vital to life. Some scientists believe that the story of their formation may have gone like this.

When the rock crust of the new planet Earth was at last cool enough to hold the torrents of rain which fell, enormous oceans and mighty rivers filled its rock dents and hollows. Some of the rocks still hissed with heat, but steam no longer gushed skyward to create dark rain clouds as it had for centuries. The clouds thinned to wisps, and some days the sun shone through.

Night and day, swift rivers and the forces of the weather—the cold and the heat, the wind and the rain and snow—worked to break the rocks into smaller and smaller pieces. Down the mountains rushed the rivers to the sea, dragging stones of all sizes that had been worn loose from the rock. Gradually, the sea bottom began to build up with these specks and grains—the first soil.

At first, there was nothing alive. Life needed a long time to develop. At last, about a billion years ago, sponges, worm-like creatures and tiny shelled animals were born in the shallows of the oceans. When these creatures died, their bodies dropped to the bottom and mixed with the dirt and gravel the rivers were washing into the ocean.

The first plants sprouted in this soil about 360 million

years ago. They were very weak and small, and their roots were not strong enough to support them. But the soil had been enriched with decomposing bodies of floating plants and animals. As new generations of plants evolved, their roots grew stronger. They spread out like fingers, clutching the soil with runners.

When they died, their leaves and roots rotted, enriching the bottom muck. Stronger, taller plants grew in the richer soil and their roots captured more soil. At last, about 300 million years ago, plants grew so thickly, their tangle of roots so dense, that some shallow areas of the ocean became something new—marshy land. The first wetlands had been born.

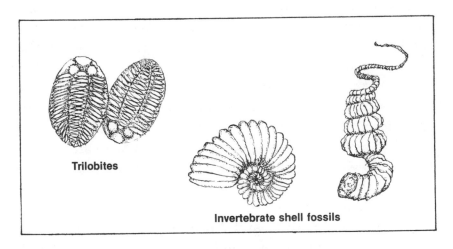

Trilobites

Invertebrate shell fossils

These are the fossils of some of the first shelled animals who lived in the shallow parts of the ocean.

Plants grew well in the warm squishy earth. After many years and many generations of plants, huge ferns pushed their fiddleheads out of trunks taller than a three-story house! Club mosses and gigantic ground pines arched their feathery branches like great beach umbrellas. The air must have smelled of growing and decay, like woods' earth in spring.

As millions of years passed, the earth continued to change. Seawater washed over sinking land, and then withdrew when land was pushed into mountains by forces deep inside the earth. Sometimes thick swamp forests covered low land all over the earth. Sometimes earthquakes crumpled the earth's surface or volcanoes vomited molten rock, burying entire swamps. In some places, swamp forests were buried with mud and sand, forcing the layers of decaying plants and animals close together. After many centuries, the buried, pressed muck crumbled into a mossy substance we call "peat."

Pushed far underground, some layers of peat were baked solid by the terrible heat that comes up into the rocks from deep in the earth. The peat was pressed and baked until what remained was a form of carbon we call "coal." Geologists who study the earth's rocks estimate that rotting wetland life, five to eight feet thick, was compressed into only one foot of coal.

All over Europe and North America, people have heated their homes with chunks of peat and coal. Coal is sometimes called "buried sunshine" because it is made from living things which were made with the help of energy in sunlight. Coal is trapped energy from the sunlight that warmed prehistoric swamps. It is fascinating to think we can be warm in the twentieth century with what is left of wetland plants and animals that died 250 million years ago.

The earth continued to change. Deserts grew and then were buried, mountains rose and then were worn away, hot places turned cold for thousands of years. Many plant and animal species died out, but one water-loving species learned to adapt to the changed conditions. The amphibians became so good at living on land that some of their later generations slowly adapted and changed into land animals —the reptiles.

When the climate became hot and sticky once more, swamps again covered much of North America. In these wetlands, 170 million years ago, lived the largest of all reptiles, the dinosaurs. Some dinosaurs had long swaying necks and bony little heads. Others walked on their hind legs and stood as tall as trees. In the leaves of gigantic tree ferns, the first true bird, about the size of a pigeon, pulled itself along with the help of claws on its wings. It could not yet fly.

One muggy day, an enormous dinosaur, Brontosaurus, the "Thunder Lizard," waded slowly out of the plant-choked lake to lay her eggs in the mud. Brontosaurus was a plant-eater, an herbivore, and was very gentle. The swamp, with its lush, leafy plants was a perfect place for her to live. Weighing more than ten elephants and almost as long as an Olympic-sized swimming pool, she needed lots of leafy plants to eat and water to support her heavy body.

As she pushed the mud awkwardly over her eggs

with her huge, elephant-like foot, she turned her head toward a noise and saw another dinosaur, Allosaurus, whose name means "leaping reptile." It came lumbering toward her on his strong hind legs. Allosaurus was a meat-eater, a carnivore, and he liked nothing better than chunks of warm dinosaur meat.

Brontosaurus was very slow on land. In two leaps, Allosaurus was on her back sinking his sharp, six-inch teeth into her leathery shoulder. When his teeth struck her bone, one of them broke off and fell into the water.

The great beasts wrestled in the slippery muck. The plant-eater whipped her great tail around and knocked the hunter away. Then she plunged into the water where she would be safe. But Allosaurus leaped, clutching her back with sharp front claws and sinking his teeth into her neck.

Brontosaurus didn't have a chance. But she got her revenge. As she sank into the swamp, she pushed her full weight against her killer. He fell, too, pinned down in the muck beneath her. Soon the tea-colored water covered them both.

Gradually, the dead swamp monsters decayed and their bones settled into the mud. Centuries later, pressed between blankets of swamp mud and sand, they petrified, which means their bones turned to stone.

Changes in the land around them caused the wetland to drain. Other changes eventually forced the rocks containing their skeletons up to the surface once more. Millions of years later, paleontologists would find their fossilized bones embedded in rocks in Wyoming. They would even find the leaping reptile's broken tooth.

Brontosaurus plunged into the water, but Allosaurus leaped, clutching her back with his sharp front claws and sinking his teeth into her neck.

Later, swamps were home to different kinds of dinosaurs. Some had flat, horny, duck-bill jaws and two thousand teeth for chewing up swamp plants. They could escape their fierce, meateating enemies by filling their hollow skulls with air and hiding under water.

Some of these huge wetland residents could escape their enemies, but at last the earth itself may have become an enemy. Perhaps the climate grew colder, wetlands dried up and the huge reptiles couldn't find enough to eat. Or it may be that a new species of animal, the mammal, ancestor of many of the animals living today, ate the dinosaurs' eggs. Although no one knows exactly why, the last of the dinosaurs died about sixty million years ago.

Many of our modern wetlands have also been formed as a result of great changes occurring on the earth. They formed where hollows were scraped by glaciers or when glacier meltwater caused the sea to rise, filling inland valleys. These later wetlands developed by the same slow process as had the first wetlands. Plants rooted on the edges of still, shallow lakes or along the banks of slow-moving rivers.

The three forms of modern wetlands—bogs, marshes and swamps—differ from one another in appearance as well as in the kinds of plants and animals that live in them. Each wetland has its own story to tell about its ancient origin, its unique wildlife and about the people who explored or exploited it.

---

3 Life in A Bog

Our oldest wetlands are bogs. They have usually formed in areas where glaciers covered the surface of the earth during the last Ice Age, which ended about 9,000 years ago. In the United States, many glacier-formed bogs are in the Northeast, around the Great Lakes and in Alaska.

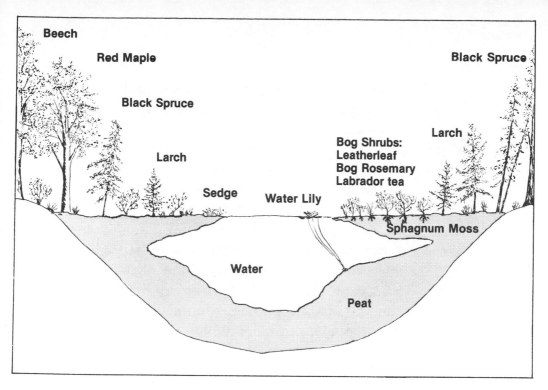

Cross-section of a bog.

As the glacier inched down the mountain, a jagged boulder broke loose, became embedded in the ice and gouged a deep cut in the ground. Thousands of years later when the ice melted, its meltwater filled this deep hollow. Or perhaps as the glacier melted, an enormous block of ice broke off and was buried in the mounds of sand, rock, gravel and debris dumped where the glacier halted. At last the ice block, too, melted, filling its steep-sided basin.

Unable to drain, the water in this glacial pond sat very still. Mosses and shrubs, plants strong enough to survive an Arctic environment, began to grow along its rim. As the plants branched and wound their roots and leaves

21

together, they became clogged with water and died from lack of nourishment. The thick mat was pushed out onto the surface of the water where it floated, supported by air in the dead plants' stems and leaves. These began to decay, and some fell to the bottom. New plants grew in the mat, rooting in the moss which is called "sphagnum."

In the Arctic, bogs tend to spread as the water is warmed by the sun. The soil under the bog does not melt. So the water cannot drain away. But the surface frost, snow and ice melts so that the trees around the edges of the bog fall in. In this way, the bog fills in from the sides as well as from the bottom up. Once a bog is formed, its thick mat of sphagnum and plants slows the motion and drainage of the water. Bogs change very slowly.

After thousands of years of being pressed by the weight of cold water, the dead sphagnum and other plants become peat. In northern Europe, peat has been used as a fuel for centuries. Dried and burned, it has twice the heating value of wood and about two-thirds the value of coal. Great brown slabs of it are cut and carried home to dry.

One evening in May, 1950, two men were cutting peat in a bog in central Denmark. One man cut the peat, the other lifted and stacked the heavy wet slabs. The air was very still, and the sun cast long shadows. Suddenly, in the newly-exposed peat below the surface, they saw the deeply-tanned face of a man wearing a cap—and with a noose around his neck! They ran home to call the police.

But the Tollund man, as he would be called after the bog or "fen" where he was found, had not been recently

The Tollund Man was buried in a Danish bog 2,000 years ago.

murdered. He had been hung with a braided leather noose 2,000 years earlier, during the Iron Age in Denmark. His face with its wrinkled forehead, even his eyebrows and a stubble of hair on his chin, were perfectly preserved! When scientists performed an autopsy, they discovered that the man was so well-preserved that they could tell what kind of grain he had eaten for his last meal!

The bodies of over 700 men and women have been found preserved in Scandinavian bogs. Some were wearing animal skins. Some had been pinned down by stakes and branches as though they were expected to try to escape. Scientists believe that they were sacrificed to a goddess that these Iron Age people believed would help their crops grow. In the bog, their bodies were tanned like leather and preserved by the acids released in the water as plants slowly decayed and were pressed into peat.

Acids make bogs the harshest of modern wetlands. Not many plants and animals can live in a bog all year around. But many animals and birds visit the northern bog in summer. If you visit a typical northern bog on a sunny August afternoon, you'll understand why.

What you will probably notice first, or rather feel, is a sinking beneath your boots from the cushions of light green sphagnum moss. Sphagnum moss is the rooting medium for nearly every plant in the bog, even the evergreens that grow around its edges.

Notice how much cooler it is in the bog than in the surrounding woods. If you reach down and touch the moss, you'll discover it is cool and moist. If you squeeze it gently, water drips. The reason the bog stays so cool in summer is that sphagnum acts like a sponge, evaporating great amounts of water, and that cools the air.

Today, people add sphagnum to soil for potting house plants because it can hold so much water. During World War I, medics used sphagnum to wrap wounds because it is mildly antiseptic as well as being absorbent. It has even been used for baby diapers!

Around its "eye," that still pool of red-brown acidic

water at the center of a bog, grows the floating mat of sphagnum and other plants. In such a harsh environment, plants must find oxygen and nutrients in unusual ways. Some plants have air spaces in stems and leaves that float above water, and underneath have different cells which absorb gasses directly from the water.

If you look carefully, you may even find a plant that gets the nitrogen it needs from the bodies of insects—a meat-eating plant! Among these plants are the pitcher plant, the sundew, and the rare Venus's flytrap. Insects are coaxed down the trumpets of pitcher plants, attracted by the purple-red veins inside. But the trumpets are half-full of water, and the bugs are prevented from crawling out by stiff, downward-pointing hairs. The sundew has sticky red tentacles on the inside of its trapleaf which glisten in the sun. As a fly struggles to escape, it bumps into more and more of the

Some plants that live in bogs eat insects.

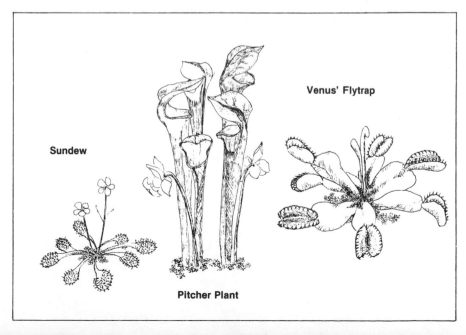

Sundew

Venus' Flytrap

Pitcher Plant

sticky hairs, until at last the leaf enfolds it. The rare Venus's flytrap lives only in warm, boggy places along the coast of North and South Carolina. Inside, it has tiny hairs which, when touched, cause the trap leaf to snap shut around an insect. This plant can actually choose its victim, trapping only those that are good for it!

Farther away from the watery eye, sedges and knee-high shrubs grow in the sphagnum mat. You may even see the tiny leaves and red fruit of the wild cranberry—yes, the same plant cooked into sauce to go with turkey at Thanksgiving.

Even in the damp, cool woods surrounding the wet bog, only certain plants and trees can grow. Black spruce and feathery-leafed tamarack are the most common evergreens that grow here, but they grow very slowly in the acid soil. You may see a snowshoe hare crouching among the pine needles, almost invisible in his red-brown summer colors. In the winter, he will turn white so that he is camouflaged from his enemies.

In northern bogs, like those in Kenai National Wildlife Refuge in Alaska, you may see a mother moose nosing in the muck. She will forage for hours in the bottom ooze. Her calf, born late in May, wobbles along behind her when he is only a few weeks old. Sometimes he and his mother stand neck-deep in the bog just to escape the black flies.

If you meet a moose, be careful! A cow will defend her calf fiercely. A bull moose, which may weigh as much as a Volkswagen, has antlers almost six feet wide and will charge when alarmed.

This bull moose may weigh as much as a Volkswagen!

Not all bogs look like the bog you visited. Some may be shallow lakes surrounded by a dense mat of plants. In others, there is no open water at all as the lake is almost entirely filled. But a true bog is fed only by the rain. No streams flow in or out, and because it stands so still, a bog changes very slowly and lives a long time. It is like a living museum that is recording changes in the climate and plants of the surrounding area for thousands of years. At the bottom of Humptulips Bog in western Washington, botanists have found fossils of pollen grain that are 50,000 years old!

4 At Home in the Freshwater Marsh

Pretend, for a moment, that you are a boy living in the marshes south of Baghdad, Iraq. What you must do every morning in summer is scramble up on the back of your family's water buffalo, and steer her while she swims to the shallow grazing ground where the green rush shoots grow. At sunset, you go in a boat with the other children to ride your animal home. You drive her onto a platform on your island home, close to the fire where the smoke keeps the insects away. You are very careful with her, as your family needs her for milk and butter, and when she is older, for her meat and her hide.

Here, in the middle of the hot deserts of the Middle East, the Ma'dan, or Reed people, have lived for centuries with too much water. They have built their horseshoe-shaped reed houses on islands that are raised above the water on layers of reeds so that if the marsh floods in heavy rains, they will stay dry. Everyday, they pack the fish that they have caught in ice and pole their boats to the nearest market town to sell it. They also grow rice and weave reeds into mats.

People have lived in these marshes for thousands of years. This is where the Tigris and Euphrates rivers join before emptying into the Persian Gulf. Many believe that the

Every day, the marsh Arabs pack the fish they catch in ice and pole their boats to the dry-land market to sell them.

Garden of Eden was located right here in this marsh. So much water in such a vast desert was a wonderful blessing.

Other ancient civilizations, too, were built around marshes. The Egyptians were able to build an empire in the desert because the soil in the marshes along the Nile River was so fertile. The city of Timbuctoo, center of the ancient West African kingdom of Mali, rose over a great inland marsh along the Niger River. Timbuctoo was so rich and so beautiful that even today its name is used to mean a glorious, far-away empire.

Even when people were not living in marshes, they used plants, animals and birds that did. People have always fished and hunted in marshes, and marshes are still the source of the world's most important everyday food—rice. In the great marshes through which the River Nile flows in central Africa, grows dense patches of giant gray-green sedge plants called papyrus. Thousands of years ago, ancient Egyptians made the first paper by pressing pith they took from the stalks of papyrus. It is no longer used to make paper because it is more expensive and not as durable as modern paper made from wood, cloth and other materials.

Papyrus grows so well in these marshes that for years explorers were unable to trace the Nile through the papyrus jungle. These wetlands, called the Sudd, are so thick with plants that boats find it very hard to pass through. During the 19th century, a few steamboats were trapped here, and some of the passengers starved to death. In other African marshes, too, heat and high humidity makes plants grow thickly. Great bulky hippopotamuses keep paths open as they clump out of the marsh to graze in the cool evening.

Disease-carrying mosquitoes and germs such as bacteria also grow well in hot, tropical marshes. Because of this, many of these wetlands have been filled or drained. But the battle against insects was not won until the discovery of the insecticide DDT during the 1940s. Today, certain kinds of illness, like malaria, have been greatly reduced while others have been almost entirely wiped out.

In the United States, where illness from disease-carrying insects has not been a serious problem, freshwater

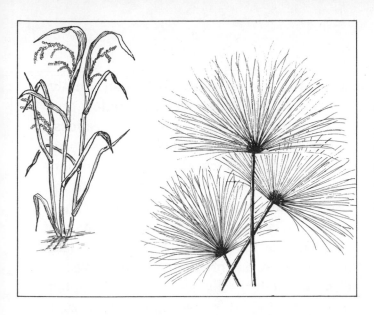

Two of the world's most important plants grow in freshwater marshes: rice (on the left) and papyrus (on right).

marshes provide homes for hundreds of birds, animals and fish. The creatures who live here need water for swimming and catching food, and grasses and plants to eat and to hide in.

In summer, a marsh looks like a watery prairie with its tall green grass. In some places, freshwater marshes are even called prairies. Wind rustles and shimmers the grass just as it does grass on the Great Plains of our Midwest. These grasses, along with other grasslike plants—reeds, rushes and cattails—started the marsh by taking root in the muddy bottom, usually near the bend of a gently moving river or in an abandoned river channel. Some marshes get started near the mouths of rivers—called deltas— where the rivers drop the silt they have been carrying before they flow into the sea. The marsh is usually fed by its river, and so its water flows, although very slowly. Slow-flowing rivers or channels through marshes are known in the South as bayous.

Water birds who live in a freshwater marsh usually stay there only part of the year. Marsh water is shallow and not well-protected from the weather. So in winter, ducks, geese and other water birds fly hundreds of miles to warm southern marshes. In spring, these travelers fly back to northern marshes, where new plant growth is starting and insects, frogs and fish they like to eat are being born. If they stayed in southern marshes, they would have to compete with permanent residents for food, and there would be less food and many more enemies to threaten their nestlings.

The migrating water birds fly along wide air paths called flyways. Each evening, they rest and eat in wild wetlands. Ducks and geese use the same paths year after

Migrating water birds fly north and south along wide air paths called flyways.

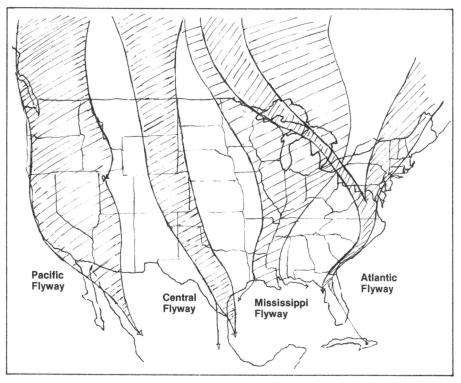

Pacific Flyway

Central Flyway

Mississippi Flyway

Atlantic Flyway

year, even stopping along the way in the same marshes. But during the last century, many marshes along the flyways were filled or drained for farmland, houses and factories. Not finding enough to eat in wild wetlands, the birds descended on farmers' grain fields. In California, ducks flew into the Sacramento Valley rice fields and the Imperial Valley lettuce fields. Hungry ducks love rice and lettuce.

The farmers were very upset. Something had to be done. They shot many of the ducks, but more came. Then the farmers hired pilots to fly low over the fields and terrify the birds. The birds would fly away—but later they came back.

At last, the Federal government began to establish National Wildlife Refuges, many of them wetlands, to protect and feed migrating birds and to relieve farmers. Now the rangers in the refuges grow extra grain for water birds, and hungry migrants are welcomed by the thousands.

Even before the ice is gone from the marshes, flocks of Canada geese can be heard honking as they fly north in their "V" formations. The black silhouette of a flying Canada goose is the symbol of the National Wildlife Refuges. The geese will nest in quiet marshes like those in Bear River National Wildlife Refuge, where the Bear River empties into Great Salt Lake in Utah.

All over the country, mating calls replace the howling of winter storms as part-time residents come back to northern marsh homes. Male redwinged blackbirds with their brilliant scarlet shoulder patches sway on cattails that look moth-eaten because they have gone to seed. "Kong-quer-eee" call the blackbirds. In western marshes, the yellow-headed blackbirds sound their low harsh warnings: "This is my home, stay away!" Female blackbirds are smaller than the males. Their brown backs disguise them well as they nest among the cattails and dead grasses.

Each spring, thousands of wild ducks return to the small pothole marshes of the Great Plains. Swimming in pairs and clucking to each other, they choose a nest site. Hundreds of these small marshes in Minnesota, North and South Dakota and southern Canada have grown in sinkholes dug by the last glacier 11,000 years ago.

Some are tiny, and are flooded only a few weeks a year. Here the mother duck makes her nest away from other ducks of her species. When the ducklings have grown a little

A male redwinged blackbird sways on cattails that look moth-eaten because they have gone to seed during the winter.

but are still not able to fly, she moves them to a bigger marsh where they can find enough plants and insects to eat. And they can escape from their enemies by diving beneath the deeper water or by darting in and out of the twisting, reed-lined channels. Prairie pothole marshes are ideal for wild ducks because these and the larger ones exist close together.

By the time the migrants return in spring, northern marsh plants are beginning to sprout fresh green shoots. Algae coat the underwater stems of cattails and rushes. Algae are plants so tiny they can be seen only with a micro-scope, yet many marsh residents, like sunfish, insects and tadpoles, depend on them for food. Closer to the mud shore, the water is coated with green duckweed, tiny plants with no stems and dangling roots. The broadleaf pads floating around them are water lilies. Their leaves are connected by slender stalks to tough stems, sometimes as thick as a man's wrist. The stems burrow deep into the mud. The water lilies' elegant yellow and white blossoms begin to appear in southern marshes early in April; farther north, they will bloom much later. Sometimes their blossoms are a foot wide.

Water lilies grow in wetlands all over the country. In fact, they grow all over the world. They are related to the lotus, the sacred flower of the ancient Egyptians who modeled the tops of temple columns on their shape. In the great flat delta marshes of the Volga River near the Caspian Sea, in the Soviet Union, lotus leaves grow so large that a child could hide beneath one!

Wherever they grow, water lilies form their own little world. Frogs and small turtles bask on the pads. Under-neath, tiny sponges grow and water mites, snails, beetles and damselflies lay their eggs. Later, tadpoles and sunfish hiding here will eat the eggs. Swans, ducks and sometimes muskrats eat the water lilies. Farther north, moose browse among them like cows in pasture grass.

To avoid being eaten is the marsh dweller's biggest challenge. While lots of food grows in a marsh, there are also many hungry birds, animals and fish. To find enough, marsh creatures often eat each other.

A brown mother mallard swims along with her eight fuzzy ducklings paddling hard to keep up with her. Suddenly the last duckling in line disappears beneath the water, leaving only rings. A snapping turtle weighing as much as a three-year-old child has gobbled it down.

Frogs and toads must lay many, many eggs because turtles, herons, water snakes, fish and dragonfly nymphs eat either the eggs or the newborn tadpoles. The spring peeper, a tiny tree frog, lays 800 eggs, the big bullfrog as many as 20,000.

Brightly colored insects dart through the air above the marsh searching for mosquitoes and flies to eat. When they pause to rest, you can see their transparent patterned wings. Dragonflies rest with their wings outspread; their cousins, the damselflies, with theirs folded over their backs. Both begin life under the water, passing through a water nymph stage, during which they will eat not only frogs' eggs and tadpoles, but anything smaller than they, including fish.

Frogs eat the grownup dragonflies, as well as many other insects. Their sticky tongues dart out so fast they can barely be seen. Large bullfrogs capture small fish, snakes, mice and even ducklings.

The life cycle of the spring peeper, a small tree frog who lives in wet woods all over the East, is similar to that of many frogs and toads. On the water-plant stem at left, the male peeper calls for a mate with a loud, clear, bell-like note which signals "spring" to thousands of people. When a female comes, the male rides on her back, fertilizing the eggs she drops as she swims around the marsh. She may lay 800 eggs! The new tadpoles are tiny, and many are eaten by turtles and fish. But those who escape that fate, grow legs and lose their tails. Water lily pads are good places for them to get used to the air. At last, the young tree frogs leave the water for the wet woods nearby, where they will cling to trees and shrubs with the sticky pads on their toes.

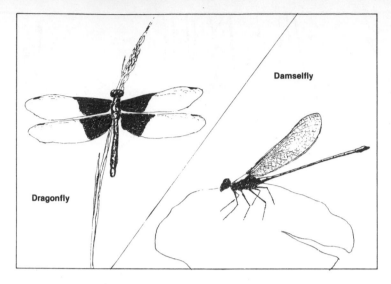

Damselfly

Dragonfly

Dragonflies rest with their wings outspread, while damselflies rest with theirs folded over their backs.

But the frogs have to watch out for owls, fish hawks, and, in warm marshes, for the giant water bug, an enormous heavy-bodied brown beetle. The giant water bug injects poison into a frog or fish with its sharp beak. The poison dissolves the muscles, bones and organs of the victim into liquid, which the bug then sucks out, leaving the skin crumpled and empty.

What eats the giant water bug? Herons, fish hawks, water snakes, large fish do. In the marsh, every creature eats and is eaten.

Hungry animals come into the marsh to feed. Skunks are fond of snapping turtle eggs. Mink and foxes eat young redwinged blackbirds and other baby birds. Raccoons raid duck nests, dig up batches of turtle eggs and scoop fish from the shallows.

People, too, come into the marsh to hunt. Because water birds nest all spring and summer, hunting is allowed only in the fall, when marsh birds are flying south for the winter. Most hunters are looking for ducks or geese in the air over marshes, but sometimes they make a mistake, shooting instead a rare wild swan or crane.

One kind of crane, the whooping crane, is so rare that hunters in wildlife refuges near them must pass a bird identification course and carry portable radios which warn them of the cranes' movements. Flying overhead, this snow-white bird with its great black-tipped wings could be confused with a snow goose. On the ground, however, whoopers with their red crown patches stand five feet tall—much larger and very different from the snow goose. Whooping cranes are so rare that every fall, hundreds of people come to Aransas National Wildlife Refuge in Texas to watch them arrive from their Arctic nesting grounds 2,500 miles away.

A pair of whooping cranes watches over a chick.

In 1941, there were only twenty-one cranes left in the world. Now, because their homes have been well-protected, there are about eighty. Biologists studying them are trying an experiment with their cousins, the greater sandhill cranes, to see if they can increase the number of whooping crane chicks.

The female whooping crane lays two large, brown-mottled eggs in a nest on the ground of Woods Buffalo National Park in northern Canada. But the parents can only raise one chick, as they must defend it from enemies for several months until it learns to fly. So in May, 1975, biologists stole one egg from each of fourteen whooping crane nests, wrapped them carefully in wool socks and flew with them to Idaho. The next day they placed one egg into the nests of fourteen pairs of greater sandhill cranes in the mountain marshes of Grays Lake National Wildlife Refuge.

The sandhill cranes squawked and fled their nests as the men skimmed the marsh in an airboat, substituting whooping crane eggs for sandhill crane eggs. But afterward, they came back. Early in June, nine whooper chicks were born. The baby cranes had to be protected from coyotes and other enemies. When the marsh dried up in a drought, they had trouble finding enough food. But the sandhill crane parents raised the new chicks as if they belonged to them. That fall, five flew south with their adoptive parents. Since then, eleven more have been raised in the Rocky Mountain marshes.

In the Bosque del Apache National Wildlife Refuge in New Mexico, where the cranes take their adopted chicks in winter, biologists have discovered that the young whooping cranes seem to be able to recognize each other. They are not yet old enough to mate, so no one knows if the adopted cranes will raise chicks of their own in the marshes where their foster parents nest.

For the whooping cranes, life in the marsh is difficult. Each year many chicks die. But these cranes need what the few freshwater marshes they choose can give them—a great deal of space and privacy and enough food. They could live nowhere else in the wild.

The plants and animals who live in each wetland are uniquely suited for life there. Over the years, they have "adapted" to living in homes that are part land and part water. They have special equipment for wetland living. Ducks and other water birds have webbed feet to help them swim and walk on mud. Duckweeds don't need roots like other plants, while water lilies have roots thick enough to stand the rotting power of water. Frogs lay hundreds of eggs because so many wetland creatures eat frogs eggs and tadpoles.

Like wetland plants and animals, the Ma'dan Arabs in the Middle East live in harmony with their marshes. They understand and accept their dependence upon their marsh. But people do not usually change to fit into the natural world. More often we have tried to change the natural world to suit us.

If there are wetlands where we decide we would like farmland or new houses, we try to fill or drain them. But our plans do not always work well. Often the uncovered soil is too poor for farmland because it drains so badly. New homes have water in their basements. In spring, the river floods more than it used to, because the marshes that used to hold snow meltwater until the river could carry it are gone. In summer, nearby wells run dry because there is no fresh water seeping through the ground from the marsh to replace dried-up underground water supplies. We miss watching the ducks and other birds and animals who used to live in the marshes.

In the Midwest, some farmers are trying to make new marshes where they have filled in or drained the old pothole marshes. They had not realized how much they needed the wetlands they drained. All over the country, people are beginning to understand more about the importance of wetlands.

---

5 The Balanced Food Chain in Our Coastal Wetlands

Like freshwater marshes, the salt marshes, which are our wild coastal wetlands, have been thought to be useless land. In many places, they have been turned into garbage dumps or have been filled so they could be transformed into land for power plants, resort hotels and airports.

But naturalists have discovered that many different kinds of fish are born in salt marshes or else live their early days in these quiet backwaters. Many more young ocean fish come in with the tide to feed. Most of the saltwater fish we eat or use in other ways need our coastal wetlands during some part of their lives. Coastal wetlands are not wastelands at all, they are the ocean's nurseries and kindergartens. Without these wetlands, there would be very few fish caught off the Atlantic coast, the Pacific coast or in the Gulf of Mexico.

In the United States, there are three kinds of coastal wetlands: the saltwater marsh, the mangrove swamp and the estuarian marsh.

The saltwater coastal marsh often looks like a watery meadow.

Salt marshes form where land is low, at the edge of the ocean. Perhaps strong waves and winds have pushed sand into hard dunes along the shore. If seawater is trapped behind the dunes, unable to drain, grasses may root in the shallows. Each high tide floods the marsh with salt water, but the dunes prevent the waves from battering the young grasses. In the United States, marshes like these fringe the Atlantic coast from southern Maine to northern Florida and are also scattered along the Pacific coast.

Dense mangrove swamps rim the southern tip of Florida. These grow so thickly that people have weathered terrible storms in rowboats tied up to trees inside.

Coastal salt marshes also form along the shores of an inlet of the sea, like Chesapeake Bay in Maryland and Virginia. This is where fresh water from rivers mixes with salty sea water. Such places are called inlets or estuaries.

Protected from the surf, communities of plants, animals, birds and fish will grow in a tidal salt marsh, such as an estuarine marsh or a coastal mangrove swamp. But these communities are very different from those that grow in freshwater marshes.

Like a freshwater marsh, the saltwater coastal marsh often looks like a watery meadow. Its tall grass, called "cordgrass," may grow as tall as a second-story window! If you stand still near a salt marsh when the tide is in, you will hear the grass rustle in the wind and water lapping the stems. A salt marsh is a quiet place. Who would suspect that what happens there every day is so important for all of us?

In each tidal marsh, animals and plants are dependent upon each other in a food cycle called the "food chain."

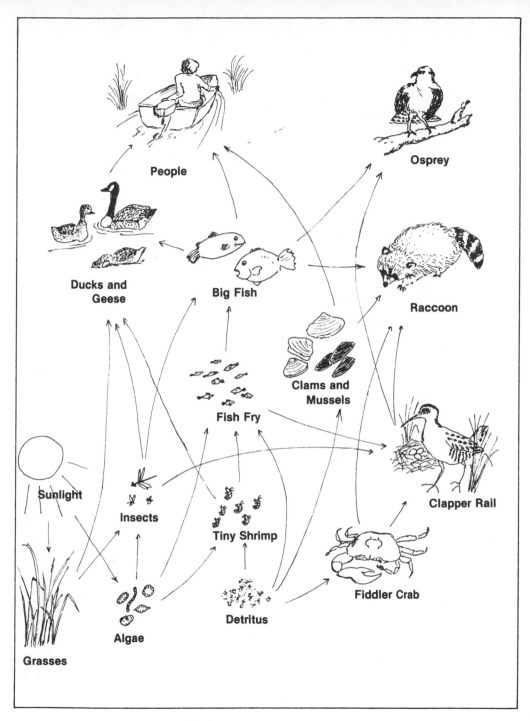

Food web in a salt marsh.

We human beings are at the top of that chain. Not only do many of the fish we eat need our salt marshes, but so do other fish that we use in manufacturing processes.

Each plant and animal in a food chain needs energy, and each finds it by eating something else. In the salt marsh, the sun shines on the green leaves of cordgrass and algae which, by a process called "photosynthesis," changes solar energy to chemical energy, storing it in their leaves. When the leaves die, they drop to the bottom to enrich the bottom mud.

Animals in the salt marsh eat the grasses and algae, absorbing the energy. Fish and bottom-feeding animals like snails nibble the dead leaves.

At the bottom of this food chain is a kind of vegetable "soup" that is mixed each time the tide comes in. This soup swirls around the grass roots, and collects on the bottom to form a thick black ooze. It is made up of algae, tiny scraps of grass, weeds, waste products, insect bodies—whatever has dropped there. These bits of matter are called "detritus."

Microscopic plants and animals like shrimp, crayfish and worms feed on this detritus-algae "soup." Half-buried in the mud are mussels and clams which open their shells and pump the soup through their gills, straining out what they need. Thin silvery fish, who have spent low tide in a small marsh pool, nose in and out of the grass, eating specks of the soup. These fish are the young of ocean fish whose eggs hatch in the marsh-rimmed bays. When they are grown, they will swim out of the bay into the Atlantic Ocean. But many will return to the marsh each high tide to eat smaller fish, young oysters, worms and detritus. Fish also eat insects and tiny crustaceans like shrimp and crayfish.

When the tide flows out, it carries the detritus-algae soup with it into the eelgrass sea bottom meadows a little farther from shore. Here thousands of oysters, scallops and other coastal fish feed on this nourishing marsh-made soup.

While the tide is out, more members of the salt marsh food chain come to feed. Small snails called periwinkles glide up and down the cordgrass blades scraping algae. A fiddler crab scoops up clawfuls of detritus stranded on the mud. Herons and clapper rails, shy, slender marsh birds, slip quietly through the grass looking for fiddlers, crayfish or plant hoppers and other insects that are feeding on the grass.

At low tide too, raccoons, opossums, snakes and skunks invade the marsh from outside in search of clams, crabs or birds' eggs. An osprey, also called a fish hawk, circles above the grass, searching for crabs, mice and baby birds.

When marsh creatures and grasses die, their bodies slip to the bottom of the marsh and decay or decompose, adding nourishment to the mud. The new plants which sprout will also become part of the detritus-algae soup at the bottom of the food chain.

Few animals in a salt marsh eat only one food. For example, clapper rails eat snails, fiddler crabs, insects, tiny fish and plants. Each food chain is linked to many other food chains to form a "food web."

Each link in the food chain needs the link ahead of it and the link which follows it. If a terrible disease killed all the snails in the marsh, it might not be very long before there were fewer clapper rails. But if there were fewer clapper rails, soon there might be many more fiddler crabs than the marsh could support with food. In a food chain, the "eaters" and the "eaten" will naturally balance each other.

At the top of the whole interlocking web stands the human being, who eats or uses many saltmarsh creatures. There may be crabs, clams and mussels, or many other creatures who have spent part of their lives there, or have fed there or on the "tidal soup," like menhaden, bluefish, oysters, flounder, scallops and shrimp. But people are really outside the salt marsh food web because their bodies and waste products are not recycled into the web as are those of other creatures. Because of this, we easily forget how important these wetlands are to us. Sometimes things we do without thinking carefully enough upset the natural balance in the salt marsh. Biologists in Florida are worried because this is what has been happening in the tidal swamps around the southern edge of the Everglades National Park.

Just as other coastal wetlands are dependent on cordgrass, swamps like the Everglades coastal areas are dependent on red mangrove trees. But a mangrove swamp does not look like a quiet grassy meadow. Instead it looks and sounds like a hot, steamy jungle. Mangrove trees grow close together, and send out sideways roots that wind in and out, over and under each other before burrowing deeply into the mud.

Until recently no one liked these trees because there were so many of them and they were so hard to destroy. The dense jungle-like swamps attracted mosquitoes and were almost impossible to get through. Few people complained when developers hacked at the maze of roots and bulldozed trees, filling in the swamps and building expensive houses, hotels and shopping plazas.

In some areas, roots of mangrove trees make the swamp look like tangled yarn.

But in 1969, two biologists, Eric Heald and William Odum, who had been studying life inside a mangrove swamp, were able to prove that life in the Everglades' estuaries is dependent on the mangrove trees. They thrive best in the estuaries where fresh water, on its way to the sea, mingles with salt water from the Gulf of Mexico. That means that the unusual birds, animals and fish that attract so many tourists to southern Florida need the mangrove swamps. Almost all the fish caught off the coast, including the pink shrimp whose netting is an $18-million-dollar-a-year business, need the red mangrove trees, too. Suddenly, everyone in Florida was interested in the red mangrove trees.

The red mangrove is an unusual tree. It is the only tree in the world that has adapted to living in salt water. Its seeds grow like long string beans and, when they fall, they either drop straight into the mud at low tide or float away on the high tide to root months later on some far-away mud flat. Some of these pioneers have even crossed the Atlantic Ocean!

Mangrove swamps cover the coasts of Central America, parts of the east coast of South America and great areas of the West African tropical coast. They also border northern Australia. In Africa and Australia, they are home to a small fish called a mudskipper—a fish that walks on the mud like the creatures that crept out of the water in prehistoric swamps to live for the first time on shore.

In Florida swamps, each part of the mangrove tree feeds or shelters swamp dwellers. Millions of mosquitoes hum and crawl along the shiny green leaves. Frogs lunge from the branches, snapping them up with sticky tongues, while young brown pelicans and egrets chatter and squawk overhead.

Each time the tide flows in, it carries a detritus soup containing decaying bits of mangrove leaves, twigs and

Mangrove seedlings look like string beans. Each seedling is a whole little plant. When its point sticks in the mud (right), the plant grows leaves from the top.

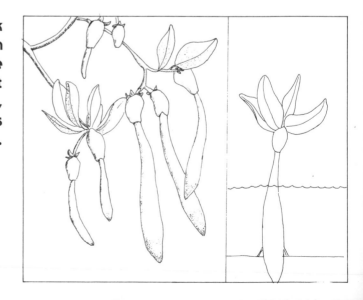

yellow blossoms. These move deep into the channel estuaries to become the food of millions of small fish. Among them are the young pink shrimp who were hatched nearly 100 miles offshore and have come in with the tides and currents when they were only tiny specks. Wading birds like egrets and roseate spoonbills search among the roots. The spoonbill is pink because of a chemical in the shrimp dinner it stirs up by sweeping its awkward, spoon-shaped bill from side to side on the muddy bottom. Larger fish, like the tarpon and the red snapper, search in the detritus for smaller fish, sea worms and small shellfish.

The large fish, and the fishermen who catch and sell them and the pink shrimp, are also dependent on the mangrove trees, for without the trees the fish would not be there. But the fishing in these waters has been falling off for the past several years. Biologists believe that this has happened because the delicate balance of the mangrove swamp food web has been disturbed.

Like all the links in a food chain, the red mangrove trees are dependent on a link—the water which bathes their roots every day with the ebb and flow of the tides. They need clean water, of just the right depth, mixed salt and fresh in just the right proportions and rich in organic food. Without this nourishment, the mangroves and everything else growing in their swamps are affected.

The fresh water that mixes with seawater to feed the mangrove trees once filtered naturally from Lake Okeechobee and Big Cypress Swamp south through the Everglades on its way to the sea. With enough water, evenly divided between salt and fresh and rich in detritus, the sea-edge

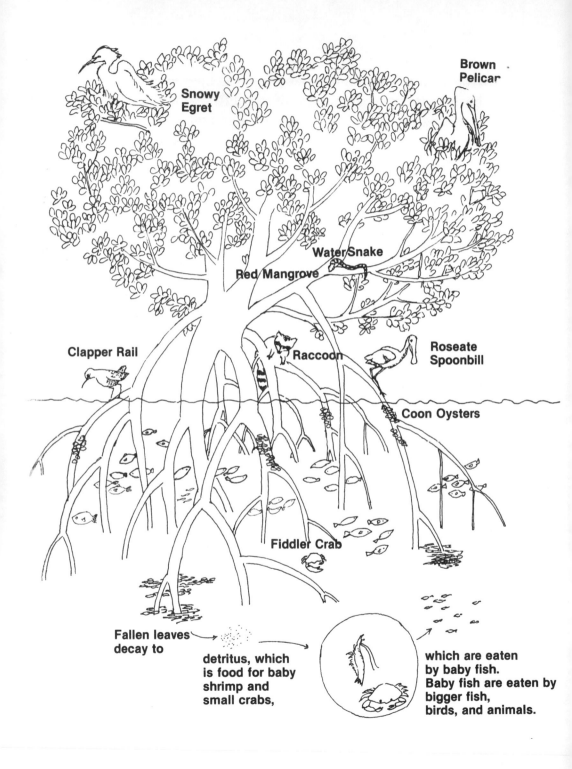

Snowy Egret

Brown Pelican

Water Snake

Red Mangrove

Clapper Rail

Raccoon

Roseate Spoonbill

Coon Oysters

Fiddler Crab

Fallen leaves decay to

detritus, which is food for baby shrimp and small crabs,

which are eaten by baby fish. Baby fish are eaten by bigger fish, birds, and animals.

mangrove swamps flourished. The fishing was excellent.

But north of the lake, people needed more water. Canals were dug to divert some of the water for farms and cities. To prevent the flooding that plagued farmers in the fall hurricanes, more canals directed billions of gallons of the lake's overflow to the Atlantic Ocean and the Gulf of Mexico. Land developers drained water from Big Cypress into canals so they could build houses on dry land.

Now, the water-flow into the mangrove swamps is controlled by a complex system of canals, levees and water

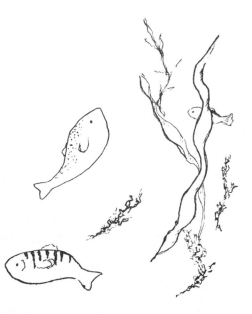

Food web in a mangrove swamp. All these animals, birds and fish, even the man fishing, depend upon the red mangrove tree.

conservation areas which are like swamp reservoirs. Engineers let fresh water into the mangrove swamp estuaries when they decided it is needed.

However, the right mixture between salt and fresh water is hard to keep up. And the canals pour fresh water into the swamps instead of it seeping and trickling the way it used to. The water has not had time to collect the nutrients the way it used to do during its slow journey through the swamps. Sometimes the water is too salty, and sometimes it is too fresh. Plants may grow so thickly that they slow down the tides, preventing salt water from coming in. Or salt water penetrates too deeply, and big fish invade the swamp kindergartens so important to the fishing industry and eat the baby fish.

These changes mean that the plants and fish that would usually live in the mangrove swamps, as well as the birds and animals that eat them, can no longer live there. It also means that the mangroves cannot grow well and support as much life as they used to be able to. This is the reason, biologists believe, that commercial and sport fishing, both offshore and in the swamps, is not as good as it was ten years ago.

These man-made canals are changing the tidal swamps by upsetting the natural balance in the food web. The damage done to the mangroves will be measurable in the fewer dollars and cents being brought in by the fishermen and the tourist industry. At last, we are beginning to realize how important these coastal wetlands are for all of us.

Naturalists believe that most of the fish caught in our coastal waters have spent part of their lives in tidal bays or estuaries—the coastal wetlands.

But no matter where you live, your life is tied to these wetlands. Even if you don't like to eat scallops, bluefish, flounder, red snapper or shrimp, you probably use products made from something that has lived in a wetland. If you have ever gone on a fishing vacation, you may have used bloodworms or sandworms dug from salt mud flats for bait. If your family buys vegetables or plants from a nursery, these plants may have been kept cool with salt hay, a short cordgrass that grows in a thick, swirled mat just above the high-tide line. If you ever use paint, varnish, fertilizer, ink, lipstick, soap or shoes, then you may be using something that has been treated with the oil of the menhaden, a small fish that feeds in salt marshes.

---

6 Stories of the Mysterious Swamps

Cypress swamps are dark, mysterious places. When the first European settlers began to explore the southeastern part of our country, they kept away from these wetlands even though they knew the swamps might be a rich source of food.

It was easy to get lost inside the cypress swamps. Sometimes the scenery changed from one day to another when an island one thought was a landmark floated away! Draperies of grey dangled from trees and brushed the face

A newborn alligator crawls out of its egg.

like giant webs. Sometimes the swamps were still and eerie, but at other times, hidden beasts bellowed and moaned. In 1791, a naturalist named William Bartram described alligators in a cypress swamp as having "floods of water and blood rushing out of their mouths." No wonder people feared these swamps.

Actually William Bartram never went inside a cypress swamp. He based his account on stories the Creek Indians told him. The Indians hunted and fished inside and knew that these were rich and beautiful places. While some people feared these swamps, others were drawn to them. They found the swamps to be places of great beauty where one could escape the confusion of daily lives and be quiet and at peace with oneself. Early in our nation's history, during the Revolutionary War, Francis Marion was one such person.

Four Holes Swamp

The British had been chasing General Francis Marion

and his South Carolina militiamen all morning. This time they would catch him. Waving his redcoats on, Colonel Banastre Tarleton galloped into the forest.

Instantly, the chase became more difficult. The forest was hot and buggy. The underbrush was thick and the trees seemed angry. Branches scratched the men's faces and pulled their muskets out of their hands. Snakes as thick as a man's wrist slithered into scummy pools.

But the men kept going. Marion had disappeared into the gloom ahead of them.

Suddenly, the horses began to snort and rear. Where forest floor had been, they were now knee-deep in thick black mud. Colonel Tarleton and his cavalry had chased Francis Marion into Four Holes Swamp.

The horses were frantic, but after their first cries of alarm, the men stayed calm. At least the muck was not quicksand. They were not sinking deeper. One by one, they struggled out onto firmer ground. Those outside reached for the reins of horses still trapped, leading them to safety.

Colonel Tarleton sat on his mud-splashed horse, looking around him. The forest was very still. Mist drifted above scum-coated pools. Great beards of grey hung so low from the trees that a man could easily hide behind them. It would be easy to get lost in this wet jungle.

One of his officers started to dismount, stretching out his boot to step onto a fallen tree trunk. Suddenly the trunk heaved up, slid beneath the black water and disappeared in a row of hissing bubbles. The dead tree was an alligator!

Colonel Tarleton had had enough. "Come on, men,"

Colonel Tarleton tries to find the Swamp Fox. The growths in the lower right-hand corner are called cypress knees. No one knows for sure how they help the tree.

he shouted. "Let's get out of here! The devil himself couldn't catch this swamp fox!"

Hidden in a thicket, General Marion, the Swamp Fox, watched the British retreat. Then he mounted his horse and rode slowly back to his camp deep inside Four Holes Swamp. He and his band of hunters, trappers and backwoods farmers had outwitted the British once again. Each of them knew the swamp well as he had lived nearby and spent many hours hunting and fishing in its wilds.

Marion's guerrilla fighters would dart out of the

swamp to raid a British camp and then seem to disappear. They so harassed the enemy that Lord Cornwallis himself had ordered his cavalry to run Marion and his bushwackers down and destroy them. But now once more, Marion was safe in the swamp and the hunters were returning empty-handed.

It would have been easy for Four Holes to swallow a whole company of soldiers. From outside it looks like an impenetrable jungle. The great grey beards that appear to be strangling all the trees are Spanish moss, not a real moss at all but an epiphyte—a plant that lives on air.

Indian legend tells of a young woman killed by an enemy tribe during her wedding ceremony. Her mourning family cut off her hair, and spread it on the limbs of the tree near her grave. The hair then blew from tree to tree, finally turning grey. The Indians believed that it lasted and spread because it was a memorial to all lovers who could never be with their loved ones.

Spanish moss never hurts the trees on which it grows because it feeds only on dust and moisture blown through it by the wind. It dangles from trees in all our southeastern cypress swamps, adding to the atmosphere of gloom and mystery.

Deep in the interior of Four Holes where one can go by canoe, the undergrowth clears and huge cypress trees tower above other trees. Along its channel of slow-moving water, tree frogs trill and hidden birds sing. Wild orchids bloom in many colors. Fallen logs, green with ferns and moss, lie in the water among cypress knees—those smooth, hollow growths that cypress roots push up in the water about three feet away from their trunks. No one knows for sure what cypress knees are for, but they look a little like knobby dwarfs.

Near the swamp's center are the four deep, dark holes, or lakes, from which the swamp takes its name. Here the forest clears, and sun splashes the water. Naturalists believe that these pools are wells which feed the swamp even in times of drought. Four Holes is like an ancient wilderness cathedral. Some say it is the most beautiful swamp in America.

The great Dismal Swamp

The Dismal Swamp sprawls across the border between Virginia and North Carolina. The great forest that covered it is nearly gone, although a few huge old cypress trees still tower above Lake Drummond which is near its center. These trees, their trunks hollowed out and decaying, may be over a thousand years old, born long before the United States. Think of the stories they could tell, growing halfway between the first two English colonies in the New World, Jamestown and Fort Raleigh.

The early colonists were frightened by the dark cypress swamp. Nothing like it grew in Europe. But they were hungry, and so expeditions were sent in to hunt and fish. The Dismal Swamp was a dangerous place. At least one expedition became hopelesssly lost. The only man able to find his way out would become the first colonial governor of

North Carolina, William Drummond. Lake Drummond was named for him, though it lies in Virginia.

Others, too, have been lost in this swamp. But some have been safe there. During the Civil War, more than a thousand slaves, trying to escape to freedom, hid deep in its interior. Many worked making cypress shingles which they could exchange for food and medicine. Some were eventually able to escape to the North.

But for others, the Dismal Swamp was the place of a horrible death. Slave owners hunted them down with vicious dogs. The slave hunts were so bloody that Henry Wadsworth Longfellow wrote a poem called "The Slave in the Dismal Swamp." And Harriet Beecher Stowe, who was famous for her novel *Uncle Tom's Cabin*, wrote another novel called *A Tale of the Great Dismal Swamp*, about a slave hiding in the swamp.

Even today, although large sections have been

Slaves trying to escape to freedom often hid in the wilds of Dismal Swamp.

drained, the Dismal Swamp remains an eerie wilderness. Strange lights glow at night, although usually they can be explained naturally. Sometimes peat, that thick layer of compressed decaying matter which lies under many swamps, catches fire and can be seen smoldering underground. Sometimes methane, a gas released when dead plants decay where there is little air, burns as it escapes. Sometimes a fungus called "foxfire" glows on a dead tree. Imagine how frightening this might be if you were lost in the swamp at night!

Even though it is close to cities and towns, Dismal Swamp remains a real wilderness, a safe hiding place for many wild creatures. In some places, trees, bushes and vines grow so thickly that fish in the water below are blind, just as they are in the deepest parts of the ocean. Black bears still hide in the thickets, although they have disappeared from the woods throughout most of the East. Here northern and southern plants grow side by side: magnolia, wild cherry, a bamboo-like plant called switch cane, and the thick vines of the muscadine grape which bear delicious purple fruit late each summer.

Naturalists and others who love wilderness visit the swamp, but few people have ever explored its darkest interior. The Dismal Swamp is still mysterious. That is what makes it so fascinating.

The Okefenokee

The Okefenokee Swamp in southeastern Georgia is another mysterious swamp. Walking along the boardwalk to the observation tower, one has the feeling that one is in a very ancient place. The air is moist and heavy. Trees tower overhead, and bird songs are far away. The swamp is quiet and watchful, almost as if it were holding its breath. Perhaps this is what the early dinosaur swamps were like.

The swamp was formed long ago, although not as long ago as the dinosaur swamps. It was shaped 250,000 years ago when melting glaciers swelled the ocean seventy-five miles inland from its present coast. When the glaciers in the far north began to grow again and the ocean shrank, water was left trapped behind a wave-formed ridge, unable to drain. Gradually, plants clogged its shallows.

The Okefenokee is a land of many stories. Its name comes from an Indian word meaning "Land of the Trembling Earth" because of the many boggy islands where small trees and plants shake when their spongy ground is walked upon.

Even the Suwannee River, which flows through the heart of the swamp on its way to the Gulf of Mexico, has its stories. A legendary Ethiopian king named Nero is said to have led slaves along its banks to freedom. Another myth claims that this river was the waterway that brought the Mayan people from the Yucatan peninsula in Mexico into the swamp where they became its first people.

Most of the swamp is now a National Wildlife Refuge, but at one time, many people lived there. Indians hiding from federal troops were safe in the Okefenokee. After they left, other people brought their families to live in the swamp because they were unhappy with changes taking place in the country.

Swampers were tough, self-sufficient people. They lived in log cabins, and ate the meat and fish they caught or raised and the vegetables they grew. They almost never needed to buy anything. Because they understood the ways of the wild swamp, they seldom got lost. Each swamper developed his own kind of "signature," a yodel called "hollerin," which identified him to other swampers. A swamper loved hollerin' at sunrise and sunset or sometimes

The swampers who lived in the Okefenokee understood the ways of the wild swamp.

simply when he felt really happy. The sound echoed off the cypress trunks and carried for miles.

The swamp they loved was still home to the cougar, the black bear and the ivory-billed woodpecker, the largest of all woodpeckers, who nested deep in the interior in the biggest cypress trees. Flying overhead, this red-crested bird, who may now be extinct, looked like a flash of scarlet between a pair of black and white flags being waved in the air.

Both the ivory-billed woodpecker and the swamper wanted to be left alone in the swamp. But other people's greed for money would change, and at last destroy, their way of life.

Inside the Okefenokee were big, beautiful bald cypress trees and tall pine trees. Bald cypress trees are also called redwoods, but they are not related to the California redwoods, nor are they evergreen trees. They lose their leaves in the fall just like broad-leafed trees do. Timbermen wanted their wood because it is a beautiful red color and extremely strong and rot-resistant. Cypress boards would make strong houses, fences and coffins.

The first lumbering project failed, but ten years later another company built railroad tracks all over the swamp and hauled out huge cypress logs. A town of 600 people bloomed on an island deep inside. But by 1925, the largest cypress trees were gone and the lumber company had left. The town became a ghost town. Rusted steam engines, boilers, washtubs, an old stove—these are all that is left of the lumbermen's eighteen years in the Okefenokee.

But the wilderness had been tamed. Perhaps this is when the ivory-billed woodpecker, unable to find a quiet, wild place it could nest safely, left the Okefenokee forever. Most of the swampers, too, moved away, although some worked for the lumber company. When the company was gone, they turned to selling alligator hides which fashionable people wanted for handbags, shoes and belts.

The alligator is a big, brown-green reptile, a descendant of the huge dinosaurs that ruled the swamps 200 million years ago. Baby alligators are born in spring. When an alligator is about to become a mother, she makes a

From a perch on top of their mother's head, baby alligators hunt for food in the water lettuce.

mounded nest out of mouthfuls of swamp grasses and plants. Then she buries twenty or more eggs. Inside, the plants decay, heating the nest and the eggs. The mother stays nearby, and will defend the nest from enemies.

Eight or nine weeks later, the pencil-length hatchlings chip their way out of the leathery shell with their egg-tooth, and begin to call a high-pitched "erk." The mother answers by tearing apart the nest to find them. She carries some of her yellow-striped babies to the water in her huge jaws, others she lures out by calling. The group, called a "pod," will live together near the mother's den for two or three months. They ride on their mother's back or crawl over thick fields of water lettuce looking for the snails, frogs and small fish which they eat.

If they live, they will grow about a foot a year until they are eight to fifteen feet long. But many, many baby alligators are eaten by raccoons, otters, turtles, fish and herons. Those that grow up will turn the tables, devouring turtles, birds, raccoons—in fact anything they can catch. In our southern swamps they perform the same function as does the hippo in African wetlands—they keep paths opened through the thick, clogging water plants so that air and light can reach the water.

By 1967, so many of the great reptiles had been killed that conservationists believed the alligator was nearing extinction. Even though they are dangerous, they were not hard to catch, because the swampers had developed unusual methods of catching them. A swamper would put a long pole into a deep pool he thought was an alligator hole. While holding one end between his teeth he would grunt, imitating the animal's deep-throated growl. The vibrations carried down the pole, and pretty soon, up came the alligator to investigate. Then the swamper would shoot it. To make sure it was dead, the swamper would chop through its backbone with an axe. If he didn't do that, alligators who had been thought to be dead for hours sometimes crawled away.

Since 1967, when the alligator was declared an endangered species, its numbers have greatly increased. In some places, they have even become a nuisance, appearing in people's swimming pools or cool garages. Some states now again permit hunting at times, and this seems to help keep the alligator population under control.

The Bayou Swamps

A bayou is a sluggish river or stream. In Louisiana, thousands of them help carry the waters of the Mississippi and the Red rivers and their tributaries into the Gulf of Mexico. Close to the Gulf are open, sunny salt marshes where thousands of birds spend the winter. Inland, where the Mississippi and its major tributary, the Atchafalaya (pronounced "Sha-fa-li") have spread vast deltas, the bayous are hot, dark, swampy places. They are so narrow that mosses hanging from branches on both sides meet in the air above the water.

The bayous are home to another kind of swamper, the Acadians, or Cajuns, as they are called here. In 1755, the British drove the French colonists out of Nova Scotia,

Canada, which was also called Acadia. After much wandering, some of them settled in Louisiana, which, with its dark, swampy land and many waterways, seemed a safe place to hide. The Cajuns built simple homes on stilts, and made their living by fishing, hunting and trapping in the swamps. Isolated from other parts of the country, they developed their own culture and their own form of English, mixed with French words and expressions.

The bayous can be dangerous places. Hurricanes sweep across the Gulf of Mexico onto the coast. Then the sluggish bayous flood their banks, becoming swirling rivers out of control, killing animals, birds and often people, and destroying many homes. Wild winds tear huge trees out by the roots.

But there is one swamp-dweller that the terrible storms help, a plant that has caused all sorts of trouble itself—the water hyacinth. It is a small plant with a pale pur-

Water hyacinths are very beautiful plants that grow so thickly that they clog the bayous.

ple flower. Its seeds are spread by wind and flooding. Because the water hyacinth spreads so easily, it has been difficult to control. Even though people have tried hard to destroy it, the plant still thrives.

During the International Cotton Exposition in New Orleans in 1884, each visitor leaving the Japanese exhibit was given a beautiful purple water hyacinth as a souvenir. Soon fountains and fish pools near New Orleans were filled with the blossoms. They had been spread by the seeds from the flowers people threw away. Birds and warm winds carried the seeds deep into the bayous where the heat and moisture made the plants grow quickly. Soon, water hyacinths clogged the water in many bayous from shore to shore. One single water hyacinth can produce 65,000 others in one growing season!

Every bayou the plants choked was impossible to boat on. And everything under the plants died because no light could reach the water. Without light, the pond weeds, even the algae, died. Then the creatures that ate plants, like the ducks and fish, disappeared, too.

At first, the state tried shoveling out the hyacinths with pitchforks. When the plants grew back, they tried flamethrowers, but the next season, the burned plants were the first to sprout. They brought in a big river boat equipped with an attachment that chewed up the plants, spitting out the pulp. New hyacinths were blooming a few months later. The plants spread deeper and deeper into the bayous.

At last, the Army Corps of Engineers decided to try dynamite. The explosions were enormous. Everything—huge old cypress trees, fish, muskrats, colorful birds—all exploded with the hyacinths and were killed. But some of the debris fell onto the muddy banks and was forgotten, and in that debris, were hyacinth seeds. Those seeds can sprout as many as twenty years after they are grown. In fact, in the year following the use of dynamite, lavendar hyacinth blossoms massed that bayou all over again.

Then during the 1940s, the Corps began to use a new chemical called 2,4-D that did kill the plants and didn't seem to hurt people, fish or animals. At last, they thought, water hyacinths can be controlled, although the state would have to spend time and money doing so. But in recent years, research has shown 2,4-D to be dangerous, particularly when used over long periods of time.

Perhaps something good will come from the hyacinths yet. In Mississippi, the National Aeronautics and Space Administration has been experimenting with these masses of flowers. NASA has discovered that water hyacinths may be able to clean sewage. On one side of a small swamp, scientists injected a stream of liquid sewage, which then flowed through a thick patch of hyacinths. When the water came out the other side, the health department found it was pure enough to drink!

NASA also found that water hyacinths can be used in the manufacture of natural gas for heating. According to NASA, a few acres of hyacinths could produce enough natural gas to heat a city of 30,000 people, a city a little smaller than Key West, Florida, or Ithaca, New York. With oil and gas so scarce and sewage problems growing with the population, perhaps this swamp plant that can't be killed will at least become useful!

Big Cypress

Along the northern edge of the Everglades National Park in Florida is Big Cypress Swamp, a National Wildlife Refuge in the making. In 1974, half a million acres, about forty percent of the swamp, was saved from developers who wanted to build a jetport. Had the jetport been completed, the Everglades would have been deprived of much of its badly-needed fresh water and most of its gorgeous and unusual wildlife.

Already the mangrove swamps which rim Big Cypress have been badly damaged, and much of their water channeled into drainage ditches. Bulldozers of the land developers destroyed many trees. But conservationists were able to convince the federal government of the importance of Big Cypress' water to the National Park, and the swamp's unique wildlife is, at least for now, safe.

Big Cypress teems with life, from dainty whirring hummingbirds tasting exotic orchids to trees that grow so thickly that, according to one visitor, you can't walk through them, you must get down on your belly and slither! But the creatures in Big Cypress are in hiding. Often you can sense an animal rather than see it. Leaves quiver, a bush rustles, a ring ripples out from a touch on the water. You have to look quickly.

Many creatures are camouflaged and blend with their surroundings. A rough green snake wriggles through a coating of green duckweed. The bittern, disguising her nest, points her bill and body to the sky like the reeds, and if the wind sways the reeds, she sways, too. Lying still in the water, an alligator is often mistaken for an old, bumpy, dead tree. Many creatures, like the bobcat and the alligator, do most of their feeding at night when they can't be seen.

Some creatures can't hide their gorgeous coloring. Even if the blue flowers of the pickerel weed provide some camouflage for the purple gallinule, the bird would have trouble hiding. Its beak is bright orange, tipped with yellow. Its face, neck and breast are a rich royal blue-purple and its wings are lighter, an irridescent blue-green.

And in the green depths of Big Cypress, the white feathers of egrets are very noticeable. Late in the 1880s, hunters invaded the swamps to catch these beautiful wading birds for their plumes, which fashionable women were wearing on their hats. Egrets grow about fifty of these

Egrets grow beautiful feathers that fashionable women wanted on their hats late in the 1880s. The Audubon Society was founded to protect the birds.

delicate, lacy plumes during their mating and nesting seasons. If the hunter slaughtered six birds, he would have an ounce of plumes, and dealers were paying $32 an ounce. After he had shot the parents and pulled out their plumes, the hunter would toss aside the bodies and leave the nestlings to starve to death. Thousands of these birds were killed, but their slaughter made many people angry. The Audubon Society was founded to protect these birds who couldn't hide, and laws were passed so they could nest safely again.

Cypress swamps are among our most unusual wild places, even though much of the mystery that surrounded them has been explained. Like all wild places today, they are threatened by people eager to build and sell expensive homes and shopping malls. But these swamps have been growing and sheltering wild creatures for thousands of years. Will shopping malls last that long?

---

7 Surviving the Winter: The Everglades and the Northern Woods Swamp

For animals, birds and fish in the wetlands, winter is a difficult time. Many will not live through it. Animals in the north and south of the United States must prepare in some way. But in the southern swamp like the Everglades, danger comes because of lack of water—drought. In the northern woods swamp, danger is in the water itself, frozen into ice and snow.

Winter in the Everglades

Sweeping across southern Florida is the Everglades, one of the most unusual swamps in the world. It is called a swamp because it is dotted with small jungles of trees. But the Seminole Indians who live there call it "Pay-Hay-Okee" —"grassy water"—and its most obvious plant is grass, mile after mile of sharp-bladed sawgrass. The Everglades' wide "rivers of grass" hide many animals and birds. They have even protected people. It was this sawgrass, a sedge that grows twelve feet high and has tiny barbs on its blades, that helped Seminole Indians hiding in the Everglades to keep out the American Army. The Indians now live in the Everglades, protected by law.

But sawgrass can't protect the animals, birds and fish in the marsh from the drought that comes with winter. Between November and April, little or no rain falls on the Everglades. The rivers of grass dry up. As the shallow water disappears, the sawgrass withers and turns brown. Jagged cracks cut the dry mud. When the fresh water is gone, most of the food eaten by the animals will be gone too, and many will starve or suffocate from lack of the oxygen they have been taking out of the water.

Early in the dry season, an alligator hole may look

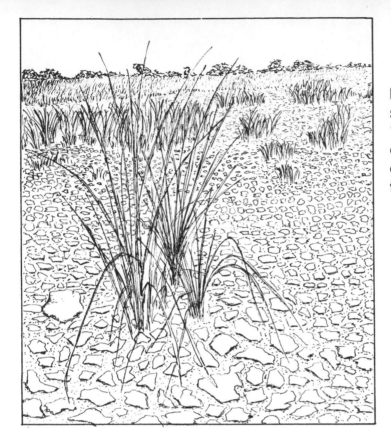

During the winter season, the "rivers of grass" dry up, and many animals, birds and fish die.

like an African desert water hole, with many different kinds of animals crowded together. The small pool of water is alive with fish competing for what little air remains near the warm, stagnant surface. In the soft mud at the edge, a dozen water snakes crawl over each other. Ten kinds of wading birds stumble over the snakes trying to catch the fish.

The pool will dry up, and the remaining fish will bloat in the baking sun. But thousands of animals manage to survive. Many birds fly away in search of water, the way birds fly south to escape northern winters. Land animals, like deer, raccoons and muskrats, stay on, spending most of each day searching for the little water that remains.

Some kinds of animals retreat into "estivation," a quiet state, like hibernation in northern animals, although not as deep. Estivation helps animals preserve the moisture in their bodies. Colorfully striped tree snails attach themselves to tree bark with an airtight mucus seal. Frogs and turtles dig into the moist undersoil. Alligators gnash and slosh out caves in the side of their pools. They can sometimes survive in these even if their holes dry up. Lots of smaller creatures dig into the walls of "gator" holes. For them, the "gator" hole is like an oasis in the desert.

The winter dry seasons in the Everglades have been much longer and more severe since the canals were built to control most of the water feeding the park. Because the normal water level is much lower now than it used to be, it is even harder for birds and animals to survive the winter droughts. Far fewer fish live in the rivers of grass and so there are far fewer birds that eat them also.

The Everglades kite, a fish hawk that eats only one food, is the most threatened. The apple snails that are the only food it eats need many plants to eat, and the long dry seasons kill the plants. Now that there are fewer snails, the Everglades kite, too, is dying out. In 1972, the Fish and Wildlife Service believed there were only twenty to thirty of these birds left.

Sometime in May, rain will soften the cracked, dry mud, and the seasonal life cycle will begin again. The animal refugees will creep out of "gator" holes onto the newly flooded plain. Tiny crustaceans emerge from their drought-resistant eggs. Sawgrass pushes up new sprouts. Soon water birds will return to spear fish that seem to have arrived miraculously in the newly filled pools.

But the dry season has had its effect. Many creatures have died of thirst and hunger. Perhaps in the spring there will be enough food for the fish, animals and birds who are still living in the Everglades.

Winter in the Northern Woods Swamp

In the northern woods swamp, the winter begins early. As early as September, the first frost yellows the ferns. In places like the Great Swamp in central New Jersey and LaRue Swamp in Illinois, the air is chilly and the sun sets early. The tree leaves are touched fewer hours by the sun, and so stop making the chlorophyll that keeps them green. They turn yellow, orange and red. Deer strip the last green leaves from the lowest branches.

As the weather cools, animals and birds in the swamps prepare for winter. Along the flyways, ducks and geese wing south, dropping down in wetlands to feed and rest along the way. Eagles flee Maine and Canada to spend the winter in wooded swamps a little farther south. Smaller birds fly overhead, sometimes all night, calling to each other so they won't lose their way.

In the water, cattails split their brown fur, loosening the fluff that carries their seeds. Migration of many creatures is downward. Insect nymphs and surface-dwelling beetles creep down plant stems toward the bottom where the ice may not reach. Frogs and turtles burrow into the mud to hibernate.

Some animals neither hibernate nor migrate. They spend the fall months in frantic preparation, searching for berries and nuts to store for the bitter cold ahead. As the green leaves disappear, bright red berries show up on the winterberry bushes and the small Jack-in-the-pulpit plants. Birds in the swamps all winter depend on berries. Sixty-three kinds of birds eat the white berries of the poison ivy plants that wind around the trunks of some of the swamps' large trees.

In the oak trees and on the ground, squirrels and blue jays rustle through the leaves searching for acorns. Chipmunks nose through the lush green mosses and umbrella-shaped ground pines hunting for seeds. Mosses and ground pines like these, now only three inches high, once grew as tall as redwoods. But that was millions of years ago, in the ancient swamp forests of Pennsylvania and West Virginia that were finally baked into coal.

At dusk every night, beavers get to work felling trees, repairing dams, plastering lodges and storing food. They have been working like this every night since mid-summer, barely stopping to eat the green plants they love. They seldom rest, but they are always listening for danger. Hearing the slightest snap of a twig or the rustle of reeds on a windless night, they slap their flat, hairless tails on the water, one after another, before diving to safety. Like shots, these alarms alert the entire wetland community.

When the danger is past, the beavers emerge and begin again. Every member of the colony is busy. Some repair the breaks in the wall of the dam. This wall has backed up the stream, flooding parts of the forest to create more wetland homes. These dams may reach a height of twelve feet and be as long as half a mile. Other beavers fell new trees for the lodge with their sharp incisor teeth. It takes a full-grown beaver only ten minutes to fell a poplar tree six inches thick.

Muskrats, who look like rabbit-sized mice, also hole up in their own lodge for the winter, but their lodges are small and poorly made.

When the real cold settles in, beavers and muskrats are warm and comfortable, safe from their enemies and still

Even though ice covers the swamp, beavers are safe inside their lodges.

able to swim out beneath the ice to find food. Grasses and sedges that grow in the water are killed by the ice. Fish still swim sluggishly beneath the ice, although later they may be suspended in it. An ice crust encases the cattails. The last ducks fly away, leaving the swamp in a frozen silence that will last for months.

But while the winter cover of snow and ice keeps out enemies, it may also prevent light and oxygen from entering the water. When that happens, plants, fish, shelled animals and water bugs must live on the air that is already trapped in the water. They crowd around the muskrat and beaver plunge holes, knowing that these permit air to mix with the water. Sometimes you can see them close to a crack in the ice, wriggling and gasping for air. When they die, muskrats find them near their plunge holes and eat them so they themselves can survive a little longer.

But the winter stretches on. Water freezes deeper and deeper until ice covers the muskrats plunge holes, too. When that happens, all the muskrats' food—water plants, roots, tubers, rushes and reeds—disappears in a block of ice. Their lodges become starvation cells. Some muskrats die, others wander on the ice until they find an empty beaver lodge thawed enough to let them enter. Tails and feet frozen stiff, they don't even see the dark, furry mink who often patrol the frozen swamp for food or the huge owl swooping through the cold air.

Mink are the swamp's most blood-thirsty animals. In some winters, a single mink will eat many muskrats. It may even attack the southern wall of a muskrat lodge which

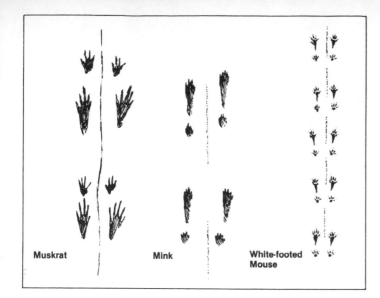

Muskrat Mink White-footed Mouse

Footprints that might be seen in the snow in a northern woods swamp.

faces the sun and so has the thinnest layer of ice and snow. If the mink can get a paw inside, it may be able to make an opening wide enough for its long slim body. At other times of the year, mink eat insects, frogs, fish and baby birds as well as muskrats.

The ferocious mink has an important role in the life of the swamp. It helps keep the numbers of other animals under control so that no one species grows too numerous. And that has been the role of the winter, too.

At last, the ice begins to thaw and the snow to melt. Slowly, the swamp comes back to life. The first "V" formation of Canada geese flies overhead, honking. Beaver kits are born in the lodge on the bed of grass and tiny roots their parents have prepared for them.

In some wooded swamps, late snow is dotted with the purple-green hoods of skunk cabbage. Growing as far west

Canada geese flying north are often the first signs of spring.

as Iowa, these flowers melt their way through the snow. Inside the stiff, insulating hood is the yellow or purple spadix or spike which is the source of the plant's heat. Bees and spiders are attracted by the purple hood's sweet smell and surprising warmth. Naturalists believe that the skunk cabbage plants in our swamps may have been living as long as California's redwoods and may continue to live thousands of years more!

In some swamps, skunk cabbage pushes its way right through the snow.

North and south, winter has its purpose. Many animals have starved to death or have been eaten by others. In the wild, those who survive the winter are the strongest and the healthiest. Perhaps now there will be enough summer food in the wetland for all the animals.

8 You and Our Wild Wetlands

It is April and you are walking along a trail in an eastern wooded wetland. Under your boots, the earth is wet and spongy. Ferns poke up their delicate, curling fiddleheads, and a trilling like sleighbells seems to fill the woods. But when you step onto a boardwalk that crosses a marsh dotted with tiny yellow marsh marigolds, the belling suddenly stops. You know you have been heard.

When you step onto the boardwalk in the Great Swamp, the peepers will stop calling for a moment or two.

The spring peepers are calling for their mates. If you stand very still, they will begin again—just one at first, cautious—but then, if you don't move, the whole chorus. You probably won't be able to see these tiny brown tree frogs perched on brown reeds and cattails. They are only an inch long, but you will certainly hear them. They sound like they're celebrating spring.

Where are you? Deep in the wilderness? No—you are an hour away from New York City, in New Jersey's Great Swamp. It is only a few minutes from New Jersey's crowded cities.

You can be in the wilderness close to city homes all over the United States when you explore wild wetlands. About an hour from Salt Lake City, you can hide behind reeds in Bear River National Wildlife Refuge. Here you can watch black and white western grebes—water birds—perform their courtship dances, weaving back and forth on top of the water. An hour from Miami, you can watch an alligator watching you with its large, unblinking eyes. You can touch the curved waxy petals of an elegant pond lily.

Perhaps our love of wildlife has at last convinced us that wetlands should be preserved. Some of our wetlands are now managed by the government's Fish and Wildlife Service in National Wildlife Refuges, but for many it was a close call.

In 1959, when the New York and New Jersey Port Authority announced that it planned to build a jetport in New Jersey's Great Swamp, the swamp was already dying. Almost unnoticed, it was littered with a sodden mass of strewn papers, plastic jugs and junked cars. But nature lovers decided that the swamp was valuable to them and banded together to raise money. They bought many acres of the swamp which they then gave to the federal government for a national wildlife preserve. Four Holes Swamp in South Carolina, the beautiful swamp where Francis Marion hid from the British in the Revolutionary War, was saved only after lumbermen had already cut many trees.

If we destroy our wetlands, there will be fewer fish swimming in the ocean and fewer birds flying over our heads. Conservationists try to convince state governments to

The swamp was already dying.

pass strong laws preserving wetlands. Not only are the wetlands refuges for migrating birds and nurseries for many kinds of fish, they also act like giant sponges, regulating our most important natural resource—our fresh water.

During heavy rains, wetlands hold back water so that rain-swollen rivers have time to carry their extra loads to the sea without flooding. Ecologists believe that the reason the Upper Souris River in North Dakota flooded the city of Minot five times in the seven years between 1969 and 1976 was because farmers to the north had been filling in the marshes along the river.

Wetlands also help regulate our drinking water.

Much of the earth's fresh water is stored underground below what is called the water table. The water table is the level in the ground at which water may be found. Water travels underground, trickling into city reservoirs. In wet weather, wetlands hold back excess water, but in dry weather, water is allowed to drip into the dwindling supply of ground water as though a matted sponge were being gently squeezed.

Wetlands also help purify our drinking water even before it reaches the reservoirs. Water which has filtered through a swamp is much cleaner than it was when it entered. Some scientists believe that if wetlands near cities are kept healthy, cities would be guaranteed safe drinking water. In Florida, for example, the fresh water in Big Cypress and the Everglades prevents salt water from the Gulf of Mexico from seeping into the drinking water.

Despite the importance of wetlands to our water supply, they remain in great danger all over the country. The battle to save Big Cypress Swamp from developers' bulldozers is still being fought. In Louisiana, engineers want to dredge and drain the swamps near the mouth of the Atchafalaya River for greater flood control. But scientists believe that the swamps themselves are natural flood controllers. And naturalists point out that these swamps are the breeding grounds for thousands of food fish and feeding stops or winter homes for millions of migrating birds.

We need to be very careful of our wetlands. Life there is fragile, and what harms wetlands can harm us all. In some places, swamps and marshes have been sprayed with insecticides to kill insects. But the insects that live in wetlands are close to the bottom of a complex food chain which ends with people. The poison in the spray lasts and lasts, and it is carried through the food chain with greatly increased power.

Before 1950, thousands of grebes lived in the marshes near Clear Lake in California. The lake was sprayed to kill gnats and thousands of birds died. For the next ten years, not one single baby grebe was born! When scientists studied the marshes, they discovered that the grebes' favorite food fish, the sunfish, were carrying 12,000 times the concentration of pesticide originally sprayed on the gnats.

Those sprayed gnats were a link in the food chain. Suppose fish other than sunfish had eaten them—trout or flounder which people enjoy eating. Or suppose the insecticide had filtered through the ground the way wetlands' water does during a dry summer, and had become part of the underground water which fills a city's reservoir. What a terrible effect spraying those annoying gnats might have had!

In the salt hay marsh meadows along the Atlantic Ocean in southern New Jersey, scientists have developed a safer, more natural way to kill mosquitoes. Ditches are dug in the mud from the high tide line into the marshes so that small fish can swim through them into the pools where mosquitoes lay their eggs. Scientists knew this would work because of what they learned in Corkscrew Sanctuary, a part of Big Cypress Swamp where people can walk through on boardwalks. There are very few mosquitoes to bother them because the swamp is also home to tiny fish called gambusia, or mosquito fish, who eat mosquito eggs and larvae.

To learn more about the relationship between our natural world and us, ecologists spend many hours studying these unique wild communities. In many of our wetlands, rare or endangered species of plants and animals like the Venus's flytrap and the whooping crane have found safe hiding places. Botanists study wetlands because they often contain plants growing side by side that do not usually grow in the same place. Big Thicket, near Beaumont, Texas, is home to some plants that usually live in the tropics, some that live in the desert and some that usually grow in the Appalachian Mountains many, many miles east of Texas! And some people believe that deep inside Big Thicket's wild wetlands there are still a few beautiful ivory-billed woodpeckers.

By studying wetlands, scientists are also learning about the great slow changes that happen on our earth. The same natural process that formed the first swamp forests is still at work. Lakes are always dying little by little, as purple-streaked skunk cabbage and grasses crowd their shallows. Lakes become wetlands, and those wetlands fill slowly with rotting blossoms, twigs and leaves. Eventually wetlands will become dry land.

The process may begin all over again when water engulfs a sandy hollow. In New Jersey, men building a highway across the salt meadows near Hackensack found white cedar logs buried ten feet deep. Ecologists believe that these cedars had grown in a bog for more than three hundred years. The trees were killed when seawater flooded the bog. After they fell, they were buried with silt. Reeds and saltwater grasses grew up over them.

If you sit quietly, you will notice small plants and animals who share this earth with you.

When you enter a wetland to study our changing earth, or just to explore, be careful not to hurt what grows there. In some wildlife refuges, boardwalks wind among the grasses and trees so that you can walk deep into the marsh. Naturalists show films, and explain the processes and natural interactions between water, plants and animals which keep wetlands healthy. In some wetlands like the Okefenokee and Four Holes, going by canoe is the best way to explore. It's a good idea to wear a long-sleeved shirt and to bring bug repellent as protection from insects.

The chances are good that a small wetland grows close to your home. If you sit very still there, you will begin to notice many small plants and creatures, like salamanders, dragonflies and delicate ferns that share this earth with you. If we are careful of these unusual wild communities, they will still be there for our children and grandchildren to enjoy as much as we do.

Places to Enjoy Wetlands

Aransas National Wildlife Refuge — Texas
Bear River National Wildlife Refuge — Utah
Big Cypress — Corkscrew Sanctuary — Florida
Blackwater National Wildlife Refuge — (Chesapeake Bay)
  Maryland
Bosque del Apache National Wildlife Refuge — New
  Mexico
Dismal Swamp National Wildlife Refuge — Virginia
Eastern Neck (Chesapeake Bay) — Maryland
Everglades National Park — Florida
Four Holes — South Carolina
Great Swamp National Wildlife Refuge — New Jersey
Kenai National Wildlife Refuge — Alaska
Moosehorn National Wildlife Refuge — Maine
Okefenokee National Wildlife Refuge — Georgia
Reelfoot National Wildlife Refuge — Tennessee

And many, many others in every state and country.

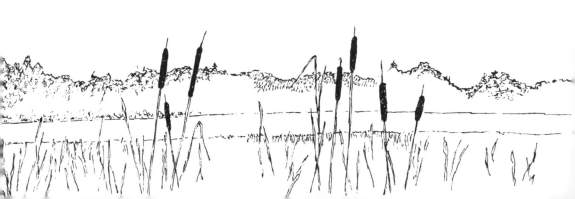

Index